Copyright © 2021 Clavis Publishing Inc., New York

Originally published as *Wilde dieren van de Savanne.*
Dierenprentenboek met verhalen en informatie in Belgium and the Netherlands by Clavis Uitgeverij, 2017
English translation from the Dutch by Clavis Publishing Inc., New York

Visit us on the Web at www.clavis-publishing.com.

Wild Animals of the Savanna. A Picture Book about Animals with Stories and Information
compiled by Marja Baeten and the World Wildlife Fund, and illustrated by Gertie Jaquet
Photos: Shutterstock©
Biocheck World Wildlife Fund: Geert-Jan Roebers

ISBN 978-1-60537-634-9

This book was printed in December 2020 at Nikara, M. R. Štefánika 858/25, 963 01 Krupina, Slovakia.

First Edition
10 9 8 7 6 5 4 3 2 1

WILD ANIMALS
of the
Savanna

A Picture Book about Animals with Stories and Information

Compiled by
Marja Baeten and WWF

Illustrated by
Gertie Jaquet

Clavis

NEW YORK

Index

Wait a Second, Little Leopard

Marie-José Balm

It's early in the morning.

"Wait for me," says Mommy.

"Be quiet. Stay between the bushes and wait for me!"

Then Mommy leaves. She crawls between the branches.

Her long body disappears and then the tip of her tail is gone as well.

I'm all alone and I wait.

Now the sun is high in the sky and I'm still waiting.

I slept a little and I played with a bug.

I'm thirsty, but I wait.

Between the branches I see the vast plain.

There isn't much to see. It's quiet and warm.

A rabbit passes by. Zebras graze and
giraffes eat from the trees. An eagle circles in the sky.
He can't see me, because I'm hidden in the bushes.
I keep myself quiet. I wait.
In the distance, a dull sound goes up.

Rumble. It's getting closer. Then the earth begins to shake.
I see elephants, giraffes and hyenas running through a cloud of dust.
Bigger and smaller animals join in the chaotic heap.
Lions, gazelles, zebras, and monkeys . . . shriek, trumpet, and howl.

9

What are they afraid of?
I wiggle myself through the bushes and start to run along.
What am I afraid of?
I run along with the monkeys. They climb up the trees.
I jump in a tree as well, and glance down.

Behind the stampede rolls a gray cloud of smoke.
Behind the smoke comes a great fire. It crawls through the grass.
The fire crackles and glows, as the grass and bushes burn.
The flames grow below me. Then it gets quiet again.

The ground is empty and black.
The monkeys crawl up the trees, higher, away from the branch where I'm hiding.
We wait. What now?
The sun is sinking behind the mountains. There are no animals left to see or hear.
Where's my mommy?
I fall asleep.

Then I hear a soft purring. "Purr . . ."
There's my mommy. I fall out of the tree and flop on the ground.
"I really waited," I say. "But then the fire appeared."
Mommy softly licks my nose. "You're a big cub now," she says.
"Tonight, you'll join me on my hunt."

The Leopard

Funny fact
Leopard and panther are different names for the same animal. Leopards that have completely dark coats are known as black panthers. On the African savanna he's always called leopard, and in the Asian forest he's always called panther.

Passport

Habitat: **on the African savanna**
Weight: **up to 198 pounds**
Height: **from head to bottom between 35 and 75 inches**
Favorite food: **gazelles and other hoofed mammals. He also likes birds, bugs, and lizards.**
Special: **he can carry prey, some even heavier than him, up trees.**

The leopard can easily crawl into a tree with his sharp claws. He likes to sleep on a big branch.

The leopard is familiar to cats. Just like the lion, the tiger, and the cheetah.

The leopard isn't as fast as gazelles. But when he sneaks up on them, he can quickly grab them with his teeth.

If he must, the leopard can live a month without drinking. There's enough water in his food.

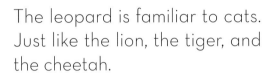

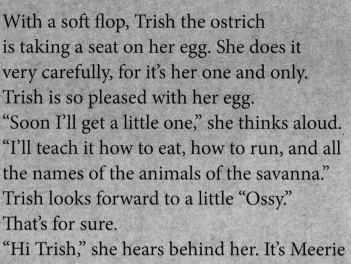

Trish's Egg
Lucas Arnoldussen

With a soft flop, Trish the ostrich
is taking a seat on her egg. She does it
very carefully, for it's her one and only.
Trish is so pleased with her egg.
"Soon I'll get a little one," she thinks aloud.
"I'll teach it how to eat, how to run, and all
the names of the animals of the savanna."
Trish looks forward to a little "Ossy."
That's for sure.
"Hi Trish," she hears behind her. It's Meerie
the meerkat and she doesn't seem all too happy.
"Hi Meerie, what's the matter?" Trish asks.

"I just wanted a glimpse of your egg," Meerie says.
"I would've liked some little ones, but that didn't work out this year."
"Unfortunately, Meerie, I can't let you glimpse," Trish says. "The egg needs
to stay warm. But after Ossy comes out, you may stop by every single day!"
"Oh, that will be too long," Meerie sighs. She's disappointed and walks away.

Trish sits proudly on her egg. She needs to keep it very warm, so that it'll come out soon.

But . . . she forgot what it looks like. It was big and beautiful . . . but how beautiful?

Maybe she should take a quick look!

Carefully, Trish stands up and then . . . she only sees a hole in the ground!

A hole in the place where the egg is supposed to be. Trish is shocked and sad at the same time.

Who stole her egg? It must be an animal that burrows holes, she thinks.

Trish knows that Meerkat, Springhare, and Aardvark burrow holes.

Meerkat wouldn't do it, she's Trish's best friend. So, Trish decides to visit Springhare first.

"Me? An egg? Oh no," Springhare says. "Good luck with searching, Trish!"

Then it must be Aardvark, Trish thinks angrily. But Aardvark doesn't know either.

"A little farther up, I heard someone sing a happy song," he says.

"Maybe you should check it out."

Trish searches. Soon she hears a happy voice.
Is the voice coming from under her feet?
It's singing: "I've got an egg, I've got an egg, I've got an egg! Egg! Egg!"
Aha, Trish thinks. There's the thief!
She presses her ear against the sand to hear better.
 Trish walks towards the sound with her ear close to the ground.
The sound is getting louder: "I've got an egg, I've got an egg, I've got an egg! Egg! Egg!"
When the voice is under her, she calls: "Hey you! Under the ground! Did you steal my egg?"

The voice stops singing.
"Answer me," Trish says angrily.
But the voice remains silent.
"I warned you!" As hard as possible,
Trish sticks her head
in the sand and sees . . .

An egg! Her egg! With a terrified Meerie next to it.

"Did you really dig the egg out beneath me?" Trish asks surprised.

"Why did you do that? You're supposed to be my friend."

"I . . . I . . . I was a little jealous, I suppose," Meerie stutters.

"I want a little meerkat to teach him how to eat, how to run,

and all the names of the animals of the savanna."

"I see," Trish says. "But there's no little meerkat in this egg. Just Ossy."

"I know," Meerie says, "but . . . I just wanted a little egg of my own."

"I'll let you know as soon as Ossy is born," Trish promises.

"And then you can help me teach the little one how to eat,

and run. We can teach him all the names of the animals

of the savanna. Meerkats know a lot of things

that ostriches don't. Is that okay?"

Meerie thinks it's a great idea!

"Can I teach little Ossy how to burrow holes?" she asks.

"I don't think that's possible," Trish laughs.

"But, you're always welcome to try!"

The Ostrich

Funny fact
Ostriches are curious.
They pick at things
to find out what it is.

Passport

Habitat: **on the African savanna**

Weight: **up to 353 pounds**

Age: **up to 30 years**

Height: **up to 110 inches**

Favorite food: **seeds and insects**

Special: **he's the biggest bird on earth and the fastest animal on two legs. He runs up to 43 miles per hour.**

18

An ostrich lives in a small group. There's only one male in the group, the rooster. The male has black and white feathers. There are also a few female ostriches. They're called hens. Females have gray-brown feathers.

An ostrich female lays about twelve eggs a year. The egg is 6 inches high and weighs about 3 pounds.

The hens lay all their eggs in the same nest. During the day, one of the hens sits on the egg. At night, the rooster takes over.

A baby ostrich is covered with down feathers. The real feathers start to grow when the chicks are a couple of months old. Young ostriches stay together in a group.

The Crocodile Bridge
Bo Buijs

One day, Springhare thinks of his good friend Ground Squirrel.
"I would like to see him again," he thinks aloud.
"You know what? Tomorrow I'm going out on a trip. Then I can drop in." And so it happens.
It's a long journey that Springhare has to make. But when he's close to his friend's burrow,
he runs up against a river. It's a wide, fast-running river. Springhare is a good jumper.
In fact, a very good jumper. But even he won't make it across the stream.
"How do I ever get there?" he wonders.

Then he sees Impala. She's drinking on the shore of the river.
"Hey Impala," Springhare shouts. "Can I sit on your back?
Then you could take me across the river. I want
to visit my good friend Ground Squirrel."
"Sorry, can't do it," Impala answers.
"I'm scared of Crocodile. He lives in the river.
And if I'm not very careful,
he'll eat me, from horn to tail."
"But you're the best runner," Springhare says.
"Crocodile will never catch us
if we run as fast as we can."

But Impala doesn't listen. She walks away, leaving Springhare alone.
Not long after, Snake crawls along.
"Hey Snake," Springhare says. "Can I sit on your back?
Then you can take me across the river.
I want to visit my good friend Ground Squirrel."
"Sorry, can't do it," Snake answers. "I'm scared of Crocodile.
He lives in the river. And if I'm not very
careful, he'll eat me, from head to tail."
"But you're the best slider," Springhare says.
"Crocodile will never catch us if we slide as fast as we can."
But Snake doesn't listen. He crawls away, leaving Springhare alone.
He sighs. No one will help me, he thinks. Then he sees Turtle.
"Hey Turtle," he shouts. "I need to get across the stream.
Can I sit on your belly? Then we can float on the water
to the other side."
"Sorry, can't do it," Turtle says. "I'm scared of Crocodile.
He lives in the river. And if I'm not very careful, he'll eat me, shell and all."
"But I can peddle with my paws," Springhare says.

"Crocodile will never catch us if we float as fast as we can."
Turtle shakes his head. He walks away
and leaves Springhare behind.

Then Springhare hears chatter. It's a flock of weaverbirds. One of them sits close to Springhare. "Hey Birdy!" Springhare says. "I need to get across the river. I want to visit my good friend Ground Squirrel. Can I sit on your back? Then you can take me to the other side."

Birdy hops to Springhare. "Sorry, can't do it," she says. "I'm scared of Crocodile. If I'm not very careful, he'll eat me, feathers and all."

"But you can fly so high," Springhare says. "We'll fly so high that Crocodile won't catch us."

"With you on my back, I'll easily crash," Birdy says. She flies away and leaves Springhare behind.

Now I'm really going home, he thinks sadly. I'll never make it across the river.

Suddenly Springhare hears someone smacking. It's Crocodile.
He's hungry for Springhare, that's for sure.
But Springhare isn't scared. He has an idea.
"Dear Crocodile," he says. "Everybody is afraid of you. Did you know that?"
Crocodile smiles. "Of course they're afraid of me. I'm big and dangerous."
He shows his big teeth. He has a lot of them. They're sharp and they're shining in the sun.
"Your teeth look quite dangerous," Springhare cheerfully says. "But you aren't that big."
"Not that big?" Crocodile says. "I'm the biggest crocodile in Africa."
"Then lay your head on this side of the water," Springhare says.
"And lay the tip of your tail on the other side. I bet you won't make it!"

Crocodile starts to laugh.
He does what Springhare asks: he lays his head on one side of the water
and his tail on the other side. "You see? Easy," he brags.
But that smart Springhare can't hear him anymore.
He quickly hops over Crocodile to the other side
of the water, where Ground Squirrel is waiting for him.
And they have a very nice time.

The Nile Crocodile

Passport

Habitat: **in the African rivers and swamps**
Weight: **up to 1540 pounds**
Height: **about 140 to 235 inches**
Favorite food: **fish and mammals**
Special: **his long, strong beak**

Funny fact

Crocodiles are one of the oldest animals on earth. They've been here since the time of dinosaurs!

The crocodile is a reptile, just like a snake and a turtle. The little ones come from an egg. The shell of a crocodile's egg is not hard, but tough.

Mother crocodile can't breed the eggs, because she's a coldblooded animal. She often lays the eggs in a hole in the sand.

When a crocodile gets hot, he opens his beak. Cold air blows through his mouth.

Sometimes a crocodile eats a big animal, like a wildebeest. After that, the crocodile doesn't have to eat for months.

Pumba Is So Tired

Saskia Goldschmidt

The elephant herd is running for hours over the savanna, in the burning sun. Pumba, the baby elephant, stays still. She's wheezy and tired. The other elephants, the aunts, the nephews, and the nieces, pass her. So does her brother, Tootie. He walks with his head raised. He wants to be part of the big ones. Tootie is already three years old and doesn't want to drink from Mommy anymore, but that doesn't mean that he has to be rude! Some aunts gently trump as if to say: Come on, little one, walk along! But Pumba is exhausted. Mommy stays behind her and softly pushes her head against Pumba. Pumba turns around and goes to Mommy's belly. She wants to drink! Mommy does one step backwards, so that Pumba can't reach her. Then she puts her trunk in the air and trumps so hard that Ooma, the oldest elephant of the herd, can hear her from all the way in the front. It means: We have to pause!

The whole herd stays still as Ooma stops. She's the boss. She's the oldest and she's very wise. She also has the biggest tusks of all females. Ooma slowly walks toward Mommy and Pumba. The other elephants follow her. Now they're standing in a circle around Pumba and Mommy.

Except for Tootie and some other tough boys. They're waiting a little further, while they flap their ears to cool down a bit.
"What's wrong?" Ooma asks, while she looks Pumba in the eyes. "I'm so tired," Pumba answers. She shyly shakes her tail and head.

"I see," Ooma says. "But we can't stay here for too long. We must go to the watering place. There's a big puddle nearby, no more than a thirty-minute walk, with enough water for us all. We can drink there and give each other a nice shower. We can also eat from the trees on the edge of the watering place. That's why we have to keep on moving. Do you understand?" "Yes Ooma," Pumba whispers. And then Ooma gently touches the baby elephant with her long trunk, sweetly, as if to say: Hold on, little girl. You can do it. We're all here to help you!

Some of the elephant aunts caress Pumba as well.
Strangely, all the soft, warm, wrinkly trunks help Pumba.
She suddenly doesn't feel tired anymore. She can walk for half an hour.
And so the herd continues its journey. After a while, they finally see the large watering place.
Tootie sees it first, and he starts to run. The other boys run with him. And Pumba?
She follows them frolicking! As soon as Pumba reaches the water, her big brother sprays her
with his trunk—she's drenched! But Pumba doesn't mind. It's quite refreshing.
She rolls in the water until her whole skin is wet. Then she runs to Mommy,
so that she can finally drink her milk. After that, Pumba wants to sleep and dream.
Sleep well, Pumba. Have a good rest, because tomorrow you'll have to walk a long distance as well.

The African Elephant

Funny fact
African elephants have very large ears. Asian elephants have smaller ears. When an elephant is very hot, he waves his ears.

Passport

Habitat: **on the savanna and in the bushes of Africa**

Weight: **up to 13.000 pounds**

Age: **up to 70 years**

Height: **up to 355 inces from the tip of his trunk to the tip of his tail.**

Favorite food: **grass, twigs, leaves, and barks**

Special: **he's the biggest land animal in the world**

Elephants live in herds, including mothers, aunts, and little ones. An adult male only passes by to mate. The herd takes care of newborn elephants. They also migrate and eat together. The leader of the herd is the biggest and eldest female.

Males and females both have ivory tusks. Those tusks start to grow after the elephant reaches the age of two. An elephant can defend himself with his tusks.

An elephant has a sort of pillow under his paws. It helps the big, heavy animal to walk without making noise.

A trunk is the nose and upper lip of an elephant. The elephant can stroke his little ones with it or pull leaves from a high tree. He also uses his trunk as a snorkel when he's in water; he breathes through it.

Turtle and Eagle

Folk tale,
retold by Marja Baeten

Lately, Turtle is sad. The other animals tease him every day.
They think he's slower than the other animals.
They call him dull and boring. "Turtle has nothing special," they say.
Turtle wants to hide in a deep, dark hole.
Before he really does it, he catches up with Eagle.
He's big and strong, and doesn't tease Turtle.
"How are you?" Turtle asks.
"I'm fine," Eagle says. "But, I'm very hungry!"

"What a coincidence," Turtle says.
"I just made myself a delicious meal.
Will you join me for dinner?"
Eagle agrees and eats his favorite dinner.
It's a banana stew. So tasty!
"You can stop by anytime," Turtle says.
After that day, Eagle has dinner with Turtle
almost every week. The other animals are
impressed and . . . maybe a little jealous as well.
"Maybe there's something special about Turtle,
if Eagle is interested in him. Maybe he isn't dull
and boring at all," they tell each other.

Turtle is getting more at ease . . .

until he catches up with Chameleon.

He says: "And when will Eagle invite you to dinner at his home?"

"He already did," Turtle answers. "I just don't have the time."

"Not true!" Chameleon shouts. "You can't visit him. Or did he teach you how to fly?"

Again, Turtle feels sad.

That same evening, he comes up with a plan. He can't learn how to fly.

But there's another way to reach Eagle's home.

34

Turtle asks his neighbor for help.
He tells her about his plan, and she does what he asks:
she wraps Turtle in a solid banana leaf.
As Eagle appears, the neighbor says:
"Turtle had to leave very suddenly.
But he left you some stew in this banana leaf.
Take it to your home!"
So, Eagle does. He takes the package
and flies higher and higher.
Turtle thought that he would like to fly,
but up in the sky he's dizzy and frightened.
He cries for help.
Eagle is frightened by the sounds in the package.
He opens his beak and Turtle falls all the way down.
He lands on his shell. Now Turtle's shell is full of cracks.
But does he mind? Not at all! The other animals think it's interesting.
Even Chameleon admits that Turtle is quite impressive.
And since then, all turtles have a beautiful shell!

The Leopard Tortoise

Funny fact
This land tortoise is called the leopard tortoise because of the dark circles on his shell.

Passport

Habitat: **on the African savanna**
Weight: **up to 88 pounds**
Length: **up to 27.5 inches**
Favorite dish: **grass and leaves from bushes**
Special: **he can get over a hundred years!**

The tortoise doesn't mind the heat on the savanna. During the day he searches for food. He only searches for a place in the shadow when it's too hot.

A tortoise lives alone. He prefers it over a group. If the female is accompanied by a male, she digs a pit. There she lays between five and twenty-five eggs. When all eggs are laid, the tortoise covers the pit with sand.

Many animals, like snakes and baboons, like to eat tortoise. Because of this, young turtles aren't safe. They're on the menu of birds of prey, hyenas, and lions too.

If there's danger, a tortoise has a very smart way of protecting himself: he can pull his head and legs into his shell.

Daredevil Hippo

Lucas Arnoldussen

It's a hot afternoon in summer. Little Hippo is bored. She's resting in a small lake, together with her mommy and daddy. It's their own, private lake that they lie in every day. They only come out after dark, to toe at some grass and leaves. But as soon as the sun rises, they quickly dive into the water.

That's the way it is, according to Little Hippo. She always did things this way, but she doesn't like it. She watches Little Elephant and Little Lion while they're playing hide-and-seek. And she also sees Little Zebra and Little Leopard doing a race run.

"Why can't I play with them?" Little Hippo asks her mommy.

"That's not a good idea, sweetheart," Mommy says. "They would only laugh at you."

"But why?" Little Hippo asks.

Mommy sighs: "We're not the prettiest animals alive."

Little Hippo doesn't believe a word of what she says. She goes to her daddy and asks: "Why do we hippos always stay in the water? There's nothing wrong with us, is there?"

Daddy answers: "No, darling, there isn't. But the other animals disagree.
We're not the prettiest animals alive."
Little Hippo doesn't understand. She has two eyes . . . she has two ears . . .
and she has four legs, just like many other animals!
In the meantime, the sun went down.
It's time to go to land and eat a little.

After Little Hippo, Mommy, and Daddy enjoyed their dinner,
they go back to their lake.
Little Hippo now sees her reflection in the water.
Hmm . . . it's true: she has round, little ears.
And a hairy, big muzzle.
And quite a big butt as well.
Would all of those things keep her from making friends?

The next day, Little Hippo, Mommy, and Daddy are resting in their lake again. Just like other days. But now Little Hippo doesn't mind anymore. She's actually quite happy that she can hide underwater. Only her head sticks out, and then . . . she hears someone screaming.

It's Little Zebra, running as fast as she can. A mean hyena is chasing her!

"Help, help!" Little Zebra shouts. "He wants to eat me!"

Little Hippo must do something. She steps out of the water and starts to run.

She runs harder than she could ever imagine. It's true: Little Hippo catches up to the hyena!

Little Hippo slaps the hyena with her big muzzle.
The animal falls on the ground and when he wants to stand up again,
Little Hippo says: "Oh no!" And then, with her big butt, she sits right on top of him!
Just then, Little Hippo realizes what she has done.
She got out of the water! All the animals can see her!
They're certainly going to laugh at her.

But the other animals clap and cheer!
They yell: "Long live Little Hippo! Hooray for the hyena-crusher!"
And they're all standing around Little Hippo.
"D . . . don't you think I'm ugly?" Little Hippo asks shyly.
"Why do you think that?" they ask. "Come, let's play together!"
Little Hippo smiles and says: "Okay! A race run?"

The Hippopotamus

Passport

Habitat: **in the African rivers and lakes**

Weight: **males up to 7100 pounds, females up to 3300 pounds**

Age: **up to 45 years**

Favorite dish: **grass and plants**

Special: **hippos are dangerous. Each year, they have more victims than lions.**

Funny fact
The hippo lies in the water most of the day. At night they move on land to eat.

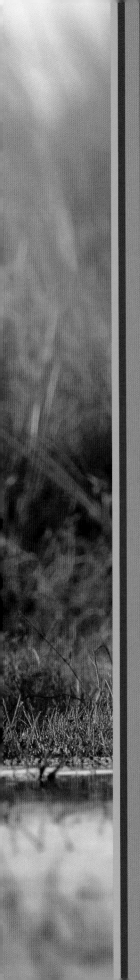

A hippo is a mammal. The baby is born underwater, and he also drinks milk from his mother underwater. The young hippo stays with his mother until he reaches the age of four.

Hippos can burn in the hot sun. Their skin is very thin and they have no fur. That's why they make their own sunscreen. This pink-colored moisture comes through the skin, and protects them from sunburn.

The teeth of a hippo are as long as your arm and as sharp as a razorblade.

A hippo seems slow, but when they're on land, they walk even faster than the fastest runner. They can make very wide bends.

43

King Liam's Castle

Bo Buijs

After a hot day, Liam the lion lies in his favorite spot: a big rock with a nice view. He looks over the savanna. The wind is blowing through his long, wild mane. First, he sees a herd of gazelles. When they jump through the grass with their strong paws, they look just like a swirling wild river. Then, he sees zebras grazing. Each zebra has another drawing of black and white stripes.

Later, he also sees two giraffes pulling leaves off the tree tops with their long neck. And he sees a giant monkey bread tree on the hill. Next, he sees three elephants resting in the shade, while a group of monkeys rest in the tree branches. The animals make happy sounds when they talk to each other. In the distance, the sun is going under. The sky is red with yellow and pink streaks.

Suddenly, an ant passes by Liam's leg. She carries a leaf that's much bigger than herself.

"Good evening," Liam says kindly. "Where are you going with that leaf?" The ant stops walking.

"I don't have time to talk to you," she says rudely. "But if you must know, it's for my nest, where I live with all the other ants."

"Just build your nest then," nods Liam with understanding. But, the ant lays the leaf on the ground and looks up with a scowl.

"Why aren't you working? You lie here often—so lazy. I watch you. Aren't you the king of all animals?" Liam proudly shakes his long mane. "So they say."

"Maybe you should build a castle," the ant says. "What's a king without a castle?" She stands on her hind legs and puts two forelegs on her side. It looks like she's getting angrier.

"At least I do something useful," she says. "I'm building as much as I can. Our nest is so big that we can all live in it, with thousands of ants. It has countless hallways and many rooms. There are separate baby rooms for the little ones. There are rooms where sick ants get well. There's a big room for our queen, and there are storage rooms, so there's always something to eat. And all those rooms must be kept clean. If there's anything wrong, it must be repaired. If there's a hole in the roof, it must be sealed. So again, actually, I don't have time to talk to you."

Before Liam can reply, the ant takes up her leaf and marches along. Then, she disappears into a gap in the ground.

For a second, Liam is rather confused. Is the ant right?
He's the king of all animals. All the animals say it.
But, what's a king without a castle? Should he work very hard to build one?
Then he begins to smile. "No. The ant is wrong," he murmurs. "I already have a castle.
My floor is all the land I can see and the sky is my roof." Content, he puts his head
on his paws and continues: "And all I have to do is enjoy it."
The sun has already disappeared. The sky is full of stars.
For a while, Liam the lion looks at all the beauty.
Then he falls asleep.

The **Lion**

Funny fact
A lion is strong and smart, but also lazy. He sleeps twenty hours a day.

Passport

Habitat: **on the African savanna**
Weight: **up to 550 pounds**
Length: **up to 100 inches**
Favorite dish: **all kinds of animals such as antelopes and zebras, but also rabbits and rodents.**
Special: **he's called the king of all animals because he has no other animal to be afraid of.**

48

A lion lives in a group of lionesses and little lions, called cubs. Sometimes, a lion fights another lion to determine the leader, and be named the strongest of the group.

The lion's mane protects his head and his neck in a fight. Other animals are quite impressed by his mane.

A male lion doesn't hunt. The lionesses do it for him. But the lion makes sure that no other lions hunt in the same area where he lives with his big family.

When a female lion is born, she lives with the same group for the rest of her life. A male lion, after he reaches the age of two, is sent away. He has to look for his own girlfriend to have his own family.

The Giraffe Is a Quiet Animal

Marie-José Balm

It has been very hot. For days. For weeks.
The sun is burning in the sky.
The last blades of grass have been eaten.
The last leaves have been picked from the tree.
The last pool of water is empty.
The giraffe and the rhinoceros have shared everything—they're friends—but it can't go on this way. They're hungry and thirsty.

The rhino roots his nose in the ground. He stomps his legs. He's angry with the dry ground and the bare tree. But he's especially angry with the warm sun.
The rhino sniffs, grumbles, and roars: "Sun! Stop it!" He rams his horn against the tree.
The giraffe stares in the distance. He does nothing. He says nothing. The giraffe is a quiet animal.

The rhino doesn't stop: he stomps and he roots.
He sniffs, grumbles, and roars.
He tries so hard that he almost bursts into pieces.
Nothing helps. The sun keeps on shining.
The giraffe stares in the distance.
And then the rhino becomes quiet too.
He's so tired. It's so hot. The rhino falls asleep.
He snores. His nose is all stuffed up from the dust.

The giraffe has no idea what to do.
He stretches out his long neck and
looks in the distance.
Come on, rain, he thinks.
And then . . . he suddenly notices
a cloud appearing on the horizon.
The cloud becomes bigger and bigger.
The big white cloud slowly turns gray and floats
closer and closer.

Finally, the giraffe thinks.
But he doesn't tell the rhino.
Because the giraffe is a quiet animal.
Then the cloud moves in front of the sun . . . .
and the sun is gone!
The rhino growls in his sleep.
He's dreaming of running around through
the soft green grass.
And then the first raindrops fall down.
It's raining!

One drop falls on the rhino's nose.
Another drop rolls inside his ear. It tickles.
The rhino wakes up, startled.
He looks around, surprised that the rain
is pouring down and streaming on the ground.

"I did it!" the rhino roars.
"The sun is gone! I chased the sun away!"
The rhino dances in the pouring rain.
He stomps, splashes, and splatters.
He slurps water out of the puddles.
He's so happy. The giraffe is happy as well.
But he doesn't say anything. The giraffe is a quiet animal.

The giraffe smiles.
The rhino didn't do anything, he knows that.
Rain doesn't fall down when you stomp, sniff, grumble, or roar.
Rain always comes naturally.

53

The Giraffe

Passport

Habitat: **on the African savanna**
Weight: **up to 4200 pounds**
Age: **up to 25 years**
Length: **up to 215 inches**
Favorite dish: **leaves from trees and flowers**
Special: **he's the highest animal in the world.**

Funny fact
Giraffes use their long necks to easily eat leaves from trees that are too high for other animals.

A long neck is also handy in case of danger. A giraffe can see a lion approaching when he's still far away. Moreover, his neck makes it easier to drink, which is quite hard when you have such long legs.

The tongue of a giraffe is dark blue and almost 20 inches long. He pulls leaves out of the trees with his tongue.

Every giraffe has different spots. On their head they have horns. These are covered with fur.

Male giraffes fight to find out who's the strongest. They hit their necks against each other.

The Zebra's Buttocks

Lucas Arnoldussen

"Is it okay? Is it really okay?" Nala doesn't dare to believe her ears.
"Yes, it's okay," Mommy says. "You may play. But you know how to find me, right?"
"Yes, watch your buttocks," Nala shouts.
"Very good," Mommy says. "I'm the only one with this pattern of stripes
on my buttocks. Will you remember them?"

Once again, Nala takes a closer look at Mommy's buttocks.
First a thick black stripe, then a thin white one, another thick black one,
then another thin white stripe, and a thin black stripe.
"Thick, thin, thick, thin, thin!" Nala says.
"That's right," Mommy proudly says. "Now go on and play!"
Nala cheerfully gallops on the savanna. It's the first time that
she goes out playing without Mommy. She's excited!

Nala has a lot of fun.
She plays tag with other small zebras,
and hide-and-seek with a few wildebeests.
When they see a lion approaching, the zebras and wildebeests
hide themselves in the big herd of mommies and daddies.
Then the sun goes down. Nala wants to go back to her mommy.

To find Mommy between all those zebras,
she needs to take a closer look at the stripes on all their buttocks.
What was it again? Thick . . . thin . . . thin . . .
Or, was it thick? Or thin?
Nala has forgotten. She thinks and thinks.
And then she knows for sure!
"Thick, thin, thick, thin, thick!" she shouts.

5

Nala doesn't have to search for long. Almost immediately, she notices the pattern of stripes on a zebra's buttocks. She follows the buttocks and tells it about playing tag with the other zebras, hide-and-seek with the wildebeests, and the lion.
But Mommy doesn't answer.
"Strange," Nala thinks aloud.

"Hey Mommy, are you listening?" she asks.
But Mommy is still not saying anything.
Nala gets angry. She bites Mommy on her tail.
Then she turns.
But . . . this isn't Nala's mommy!
"Why are you biting my tail?" the zebra lady asks.
"I thought you were my mommy," Nala answers.
And then she starts crying. "I lost my mommy."

"Oh dear," the zebra lady says. "Did you watch her buttocks carefully?"

"Y . . . y . . . yes," Nala sniffs. "But I can't remember the order of the stripes."

"I know something," the zebra lady says. "Turn around."

With a very serious face, she takes a close look at Nala's buttocks.

"I see, I see: thick, thin, thick, thin, thin. I know your mommy!"

"Really?" Nala asks. "How do you know?"

"Children are always a bit like their parents," the zebra lady says.

"The stripes on your buttocks are the spitting image of a zebra I know.

She must be your mommy!"

"And where is she?" Nala asks.

"Grab my tail," the zebra lady says. "I'll take you to her!"

The Zebra

Passport

Habitat: **on the African savanna**
Weight: **up to 990 pounds**
Age: **up to 20 years**
Length: **up to 65 inches**
Favorite dish: **grass**
Special: **every zebra has another pattern of stripes. There are no zebras exactly the same.**

Funny fact
A male zebra is called a stallion, a female zebra is called a mare, and a little zebra is called a foal.

The zebra is familiar to the horse and the donkey. Zebras live in a group, called a herd.

A newborn zebra can already stand on his legs, within an hour. The foal follows his mother everywhere. The stripes tell him which zebra is his mother. A foal stays at the herd for two years.

A newborn foal has brown stripes. After six months they turn black. A herd of zebras stay close together to scare off lions: their stipes can make the lions dizzy.

On the savanna, zebras are often seen together with wildebeests and ostriches. That's no coincidence. Zebras have good ears and a good nose, wildebeests have a good nose, and ostriches have good eyes. They can warn each other in case of approaching predators.